SPELL BETTER
in just 5 minutes a day

Margaret Harley

Please realise that I cannot guarantee your success rate, using the S.P.E.L.L Method. However I can assure you that based on my experiences using this system, and on my knowledge of learning theory, great results are likely. In this book I've shared with you the pitfalls that could prevent your success so that you can succeed. Your success will be determined by your dedication, effort and motivation.

Case studies within this book are not intended to represent or guarantee that everyone or anyone will achieve their desired results. Case studies and information are provided as examples only. The case studies described and depicted in this book are for educational purposes only. While every attempt has been made to verify the information provided in this book, the author assumes no responsibility for any error, inaccuracies or omissions.

Print information available on the last page.

Rev. date: 07/25/2017

To order additional copies of this book, contact:
Xlibris
1-800-455-039
www.Xlibris.com.au
Orders@Xlibris.com.au
513134

To Your Spelling Success!
Margaret Harley

Links

www.learneasily.com.au
team@learneasily.com.au

TESTIMONIALS

For the things we have to learn before we can do them,
we learn by doing them.

Aristotle

School

Twenty underachieving children at a Melbourne metropolitan school averaged a 79% success rate.

"*Many years ago Margaret Harley worked in my school supporting students with learning difficulties. The basis of her program was around movement and memory activities on a consistent basis and followed up in the home environment. This intervention was 'progressive' for the time as it was alternative approaches to the normal small group work that occurs in schools. Students were engaged and showed progress over time and parents were supportive of the approach. For many students this intervention made a difference and I see it as a useful addition to addressing students in their learning.*"

Former Principal Keilor Heights P.S.2014

Individuals

Love of spelling now!

"Using Margaret's visual spelling method for just 30 minutes during the week, Brooke has been consistently achieving 10/10 for her spelling tests for five months in Year 2. At the start of the program, her spelling was often as low as 2/10."

Mrs Webster – Montmorency, 2013

Instant results in 6 weeks!

"In year 4, my son Blake was always at the bottom of the class with spelling. He became easily distracted and very unsettled at the very thought of spelling. Now after six weeks he is doing very well in class as his usual score of 5/20 has gone to 20/20. We are delighted with the instant results."

Mother - Croydon, 2014

Patterns seen in words

"Amber used to wriggle and squirm in tentative apprehension of learning new words. Another avoidance technique was negotiating the time allocated for spelling to a task that was enjoyable. When she started applying the S.P.E.L.L. Method in Year 5, she was surprised that it took such a short time to remember new words. She now settles down to her spelling and learns them quickly."

Mother - Briar Hill, 2014

Spelling better in first few sessions

"Abigail has been using this method with Margaret for only a few sessions and she is progressing at a very fast pace now in Year 6. It is amazing to see the instant outstanding results which are also transferring to her school work."

Mother - Heidelberg, 2015

Homework done happily

"Harriet balked at learning her spelling and time tables each night. Now, in just a few minutes, she uses the visualisation process after writing them out in groups and colours on her large blackboard. Now, not only have her test results improved, she is confident in Year2."

Nia Ellis - Research, 2014

Tricky words learnt easily

"My son Roman is now able to spell those tricky words with ease with the S.P.E.L.L Method in Year 3. I have also used this method with my daughter when she finds difficult words. Both come back with great spelling results."

Claudia - Maribyrnong, 2015

Success each week

"Each week the results of the post tests were generally low, and now Alana experiences a 90%-100% success rate each week, using the S.P.E.L.L Method in Year 3."

Mother - Panton Hill, 2012

MY PROMISE TO YOU

Over the past 17 years, many parents have come to me with the common problem of their child's weekly low spelling results. My greatest challenge was to do something that really improved spelling results by ensuring that new words were accurately stored into long term memory.

Today, it is a different story, as improvements in results have been both amazing and very exciting.

While the topics in the book may be different, what the parents are looking for remains the same - to GET THE BIG AHA! By knowing what method can increase your child's spelling potential, you can make a decision for change.

Throughout the pages you will have an intimate look at the powerful information that has helped propel my clients to new levels of spelling accuracy. What you are reading is the results of years of hands-on work, with students of all ages, from someone who knows new spelling techniques that work. The Big Aha! is unique because it comes from both parents and students who know that the 5 steps work immediately.

Although you are reading this book because you want to know how your child can spell easily, being interested is not enough, you have to be committed. Let's face it, almost everyone wants their child to improve their spelling and success at school, but despite sincere interest, the vast majority still struggle to reach their full potential. The big AHA! is the moment when a blinding flash of the obvious hits you. It is when the penny drops and you finally realise that the pathway to success has not been revealed before now and that there is a wonderful new beginning possible. This new knowledge is here now and there is only one question, 'Are you READY to use it?'

If you want to practise straight away, progress immediately to Section 1 – How to Spell Better *in just 5 minutes a day*, or if you want background information on why this method works, refer to Section 2. And finally, for more proof that this method succeeds, refer to the numerous case studies in Section 3. These simple steps have until now only been reserved for my private clients. Now these critical steps act as a building block for anyone who wants to join my program.

Prepare to be surprised, sometimes confused, but mainly relieved and happy to know that here is an opportunity that improves your child's spelling levels and unlocks your child's potential with unstoppable momentum.

Here's to spelling success!

Margaret

TABLE OF CONTENTS

Section 1: How to Spell Better *in just 5 minutes a day*
(This section explains **how** you do it)

Section 2: Why Weak Spellers Improved
(This section explains **why** you do it)

Section 3: Case Studies –
From Underachievement to Success
(This section **proves** it works)

SECTION 1

How to Spell Better
in just 5 minutes a day

(This section explains **how** you do it)

CHAPTER 1

You never change things by fighting the existing reality.
To change something, build a new model that
makes the existing model obsolete.

Buckminster Fuller

S.P.E.L.L. Method

Follow these 5 simple steps in 5 minutes a day
and easily achieve ultimate spelling success

Step 1 - S for See

See letter patterns, chunk letter groups in colours, write in lower case and make associations.

Step 2 - P for Position

Position eyes up to the left to directly access the visual memory, and clearly articulate the word.

Step 3 - E for Enter

Enter the new word into visual memory by silently spelling it both forwards and backwards.

Step 4 - L for Listen

Listen for accuracy of visual memory by spelling the word aloud both forwards and backwards.

Step 5 - L for Let's Move

Let's move rhythmically to stimulate the brain.

Step 1 - S for See

See letter patterns, chunk letter groups in colours, write in lower case and make associations.

Preparation

Prepare a list or booklet to record new words each week and to use for the 5 minutes daily practice sessions. Keep track of one's progress by numbering and dating each list or booklet.

Booklet

To make a small booklet, cut the width of the A4 paper in half, fold each length into quarters, cut along the folds and then staple the quarters together. Write one word per page.

List of Words

To make a list, fold an A4 sheet into quarters, by first folding in half and then half again. Write one word in each quarter. Display the list on a wall or display area so that it is slightly higher than the eyes, and place to the left of the head, so that the eyes have to look upwards and to the left. This environment ensures that the words are at the correct place and height.

How to Choose Words

It is not uncommon for a learner's spelling levels to be 1 - 2 years below the expected classroom norm, resulting in a loss of confidence and high anxiety levels, so it is highly recommended that words are initially chosen at current ability level or slightly below. At first select only a few misspelt words from spelling lists, written work, or a reader. Once competence and success are regularly experienced, the level of difficulty and the number of new words can be gradually increased.

A. Letter Patterns

Confidence is fostered by identifying and ticking each correct letter in a word before identifying misspelt words. Then identify misspelt letters and decide whether to concentrate on either the misspelt letters, or letter patterns, e.g. word within words, regular and irregular letter patterns, silent letters, or any structure or pattern that often reoccurs. Here is a small list of various patterns.

1. **Common Letter Patterns**

    Identify the common word pattern in a word.

    *   double letters *dd, bb*
    *   endings *ing, ed, es, ey, ly, er, ful, ure, ould*
    *   beginnings *wh, sh, ch, th*
    *   patterns *ight, th, i-e, o-e, ough, ere*
    *   rules *i before e except after c*

2. **Silent Letter Patterns**

    *   silent *k* in *knife*
    *   silent *b* in *lamb*

3. **Words within Words**

    Often there are words within words.

    *   in *there* you can see the word *here*
    *   in *elephant* you can see the word *ant*
    *   in *baseball* you can see the words *base* and *ball*
    *   in *was* you can see the word *as*
    *   in *went* you can see the word *we*
    *   in *some* you can see the words *so* and *me*

B. Chunking

Chunk or group 2-3 sequential letter groups together, ideally syllables. The ideal size of a chunk or group is about 2-3 letters but it can include up to 4 letters.

C. Colours

Each chunk is written in one colour, so if there are 3 chunks in one word, there will be 3 colours to imprint each chunk into the visual memory. Write any misspelt letter/s in the colour **red,** as it is the most memorable and will stand out strikingly from other colours. Write other chunked letters in a different dark colour, e.g. dark purple, dark blue, dark green etc, so that words are seen clearly. For greater colour variations and gradations, mark down strokes darker than up strokes, and shade pictures using coloured pencils.

D. Write in Lower Case

For letter patterns to be more variable and memorable for imprinting into the visual memory, write in lower case and not upper case, as upper case is all one size and height and lacks a wide variety of various shapes.

Picture: Example of A4 paper, writing in red and colour blocking (shaded area), letter patterns, chunking, lower case & associations (pictures)

E. Make Associations

Associations make words more memorable and are best when they are personal, surprising and funny for ease of retention. This process engages the right hemisphere of the brain to improve learning. Stories that highlight difficult patterns and letters within a word need to elicit pictures in the mind. Examples: Let's look at some tricky words: *there, where, what* and *said*

Example 1: *there* **and** *where*

a) **Word within a word**
Look for a word within a word and make up stories or associations. The word within the word *there* is *here*. The adverb *there* is often confused with the pronoun *their*.

b) **Story**
Create a story that includes location.
There: *A large tree is over **there**, not **here**.*
This sentence emphasises position and clearly distinguishes the adverb from the pronoun - *their* - which means belonging to. These words often become confused. Expand knowledge of word patterns. A similarly spelt word like *there* is *where*.
Where: ***Where** is the tree? It's **here** not **there***

c) **Pictures**
Draw a picture of a tree to emphasise the position and interest.

Example 2: *what*

a) **Word within a word**
The word within the word *what* is *hat*.

b) **Story**
Make up a funny or interesting story about a hat, e.g. ***What** a funny feather in your **hat**!*

c) **Pictures**
Draw a picture of a funny hat to look like the letter *a* to reinforce its shape as *what* is commonly misspelt phonetically with an *o*.

Example 3: *said*

a) **Word within a word**
The word within the word *said* is *i* and *sad*.

b) **Story**
Make up a story about sadness, e.g. *I said that I am sad because...*

c) **Pictures**
Make the *i* to look like a person.

Tip
See letter patterns, chunk letter groups in colours, highlight misspelt letter/s in red, write in lower case and make associations.

Step 2 - P for Position

Position eyes up to the left to directly access the visual memory, and clearly articulate the word.

Correct Eye and Head Position

Position the list or booklet up to the left so that **both eyes look slightly up to the left side at forehead height, with the head positioned**

upright and straight. This position directly accesses the visual memory that is located across the back of the head. This is the most critical step as the eyes need to be in this exact position to accurately imprint patterns, colours and shapes into the long-term visual memory.

Picture: *Example of correct position with eyes up to the left and head straight*

Incorrect Head Positions

The head needs to be upright and straight so that it doesn't tilt either downwards, sideways or upwards. When the head is tilted incorrectly, the eyes change position and new information accesses different parts of the brain instead of the visual memory.

Picture: *Example of incorrect position with eyes down and head tilted backwards*

Say each word aloud

Hear the new word by articulating and pronouncing it aloud a couple of times to identify the letter groups and sense the rhythm and intonation.

Tip
Eyes up to the left, head straight and upright.

Step 3 - E for Enter

Enter the new word into visual memory by silently spelling it both forwards and backwards.

Spell Forwards and Backwards

Initially, this new process of silently memorising a word both forwards and backwards, may take a while. When a word cannot be recalled backwards, it means that the word has not been imprinted into the visual memory but this is not uncommon in the initial stages when learning how to tap into the visual memory.

Picture: *Example of rehearsing a word silently both forwards and backwards*

How to Remember Long Words

When a word is long, practise the chunks in gradual steps as in the following:

Example: *ele-ph-ant*

1. Write in lower case, chunk letter groups, write misspelt letters such as *ph* in **red,** e.g. *ele-**ph**-ant*, write other letter patterns in dark colours, and highlight the misspelt section in light yellow.
2. Visualise the first chunk, *ele,* spell silently forwards and backwards and then aloud.
3. Visualise the first and second chunks, *ele–**ph***, spell silently forwards and backwards and then aloud.
4. Visualise the first, second and third chunks *ele–**ph**–ant*, spell silently forwards and backwards and then aloud.

5. Practise until the word *ele–**ph**–ant* is imprinted accurately into the visual memory.

Tip
Silently rehearse word forwards and backwards.

Step 4 - L for Listen

Listen for visual memory accuracy by spelling the word aloud both forwards and backwards.

With each new word, listen for accuracy when it is spelt aloud **both forwards** and **backwards,** after you have turned the booklet over, or turned your back on the displayed list. Check accuracy by relooking at the order of letters again, or have someone listen to you. Remember that it is only when each word is correctly spelt both **forwards and backwards** that it is imprinted accurately into the visual memory. Again this may take several attempts, especially in the early stages of practice. If a word is misspelt, repeat the following steps:

Step 1
Go back to **Step 2 - P for Position**
Visualise the word again by holding it up once more with eyes up to the left of the face at forehead level.

Step 2
Go back to **Step 3 - E for Enter**
Rehearse the word silently, both forwards and backwards.

Step 3
Repeat this step by spelling each new word out aloud again both forwards and backwards.
Note: If incorrect go back to Steps 1 and 2 until accuracy is achieved.

Celebrate Success

Acknowledge success when each new word is spelt accurately both forwards and backwards, especially when in the early stages of accessing the visual memory, and when introducing more challenging words. It is always so rewarding to see the look of surprise on the faces of parents, teachers, and child when new words are spelt backwards from memory with great accuracy in the early stages.

Tip
From memory, spell new word aloud
both forwards and backwards until
successful.
Celebrate each success.

Step 5 - L for Let's Move

Let's move rhythmically to stimulate the brain.

Commence simple movement patterns that stimulate the brain and increase one's learning potential after all the new words have been imprinted accurately into the visual memory through Steps 2-4 of the S.P.E.L.L. Method. The newly learnt words are revised with rhythmic movement patterns through the following steps:

Step 1
Repeat **Step 2 - P for Position** again.
Visualise the word again by holding it up once more with eyes up to the left of the face at forehead level.

Step 2
Repeat **Step 3 - E for Enter** again.
Rehearse the word silently, both backwards and forwards.

Step 3
Combine **Step 4 – L for Listen** with this step.
Spell word aloud again, both forwards and backwards. If incorrect, go back to Steps 1 and 2 until accuracy is achieved before proceeding to moving the bean bag rhythmically to a movement pattern whilst spelling the word aloud, both forwards and backwards. The simplest and most common movement pattern that I nearly always use is the *Circular Movement Whilst Standing.*

Circular Movement Whilst Standing

Listen and spell a word out aloud accurately whilst standing still through the following steps:

1. Extend both arms down the sides of the body at upper thigh level.
2. Hold the bean bag in the right or dominant hand. Pass it to the left hand. Start and continue to spell a word aloud both forwards and backwards.
3. Move both hands around to the back of the body at the same time, and pass the bean bag from the left hand to the right hand.
4. Move both hands back to the centre. Pass bean bag to the other hand.
5. Continue the circular pattern.

Picture: *Example of Circular Movement Whilst Standing*

(Note that from my observations, when a word is spelt backwards, the circular movement reverses in the opposite direction. Usually, the accuracy of spelling lessens in the initial stages as the brain is being stimulated.)

Circular Movement Whilst Walking

Once steps 1-5 have been established, walk either forwards or backwards whilst also spelling the word aloud, again both forwards and backwards.

Test Accuracy

Test retention and accuracy of all new words by writing them down. First, say the word, secondly put the word into a sentence for clarity of meaning, and thirdly, say the word again. Acknowledge and celebrate each success.

More Movement Patterns

To vary movement patterns to further stimulate the brain. (Refer Section 2, Chapter 3)

Tip
Movement patterns increase the brain's learning potential.

Practice Makes Perfect

Practise 5 minutes a day to imprint new spelling words accurately and successfully into the visual memory.

The time frame for spelling accuracy with the S.P.E.L.L Method can vary. Sometimes it happens automatically whilst other times it take a little more effort. The greatest challenge that I notice with weak spellers is not the method but a negative belief about one's capabilities. Even when spelling is successful for quite a few weeks, confidence needs to be reinforced continually with congratulatory words of praise and reward. Eventually word patterns are recognised instantaneously and the S.P.E.L.L. Method becomes automatic.

By using the S.P.E.L.L. Method each day, its techniques often transfer into the classroom setting. Another area of change is increased spelling accuracy, as the sense that something doesn't look right develops, so misspelt words are noticed and corrected when writing stories, especially during the proof reading stage.

Trial the new S.P.E.L.L Method, that only takes 5 minutes a day, and experience success. Initially commence with four new words each week, selecting only entry level spelling. Once weekly success and increased confidence are established, increase the word total and level of difficulty.

Success Chart

Celebrating spelling accuracy acknowledges new skills and builds confidence. On the *Success Chart*, write down the list of new words, and each time a word is memorised accurately both forwards and backwards, place a tick in the column. You can also acknowledge success in weekly or monthly school tests on this same chart. (Refer *Success Chart* back of book)

Tip
Be successful and practise the 5 steps, for just 5 minutes a day!

SECTION 2
Why Weak Spellers Improved

(This section explains **why** you do it)

CHAPTER 2

Nobody without a visual memory for words ever succeeds in spelling conventionally, however educated he or she may be.
George Bernard Shaw

How the New Visualisation Technique Increases Accurate Spelling

As a primary teacher I enjoyed my work and was quite happy with the status quo – in fact it's possible I would still be teaching using mainstream methods if it wasn't for a health crisis that turned my life upside down. I was bedridden for 3 months, and could no longer keep working at a private school, but it gave me the opportunity to discover new methods of learning. Once my health improved, I commenced tutoring students who struggled to learn, but still taught using traditional methods. Then one day I heard about accelerated learning. Through the work of Bandler and Grinder (1979) who pioneered the new field of Neurolinguistic Programming, I discovered a new visualisation process. Cautiously and with great curiosity, I started to implement the new visualisation method for spelling work with my students and was amazed at their immediate and significant improvement in results.

My knowledge of the visualisation process also expanded through participation in workshops on the functions of the brain and on how movement can reduce or remove blocks to learning. I completely changed my traditional practices as my philosophy of learning and my teaching approach had changed forever. Initially it was very challenging to embrace new research and it was challenging to talk a different 'lingo' to the mainstream, but the results have been worthwhile, as I know that many of my students, who may once have given up trying at school, are now following their chosen career path.

A major breakthrough came when I was employed at a very progressive school under the dynamic leadership of a principal who wanted to aim for excellence by trialling the new research methods for Years 3 and 4 students who struggled with literacy. Financial resources were available for 6 terms which ensured a good time frame to observe the methods and collate results. These are now compiled in this book to share with you the vision of how best to assist the many children who really struggle with spelling. (Refer Section 3, Chapter 9)

It has been a long journey and it is only now that I am able to write this book, after 17 years of work. I have had to open up my mind and take risks with unfamiliar educational practices, because it is this process that has made it possible for me to confidently assist struggling students. My reward is to see the relief and spontaneous delight of both students and parents as they discover the secrets of tapping into their visual memory.

How to Directly Access the Visual Memory

The most significant research for my work was gained from the book, *Turning Frogs into Princes* (1979), by Richard Bandler and John Grinder, founders of Neurolinguistic Programming, who identified different learning modalities through the visual, auditory and kinaesthetic channels. Visual learning is when teaching and learning occur through visual images, the most common modality for learning.

Their research on the visual memory is particularly relevant to my work assisting students who struggle to spell. They identified two ways to directly access the visual memory. They are firstly remembering known information and secondly constructing new information.

How to Remember Known Information

When known visual information is being remembered, Bandler and Grinder call this visual mode of learning the Visually Remembered (VR). The Visually Remembered is activated when known images are recalled such as the colour of your mother's eyes or various patterns and colours in your home. Now the eyes will automatically move up to the right to access the visual memory.

How to Construct New Information

When new visual information is being constructed or designed, Bandler and Grinder call this process, the Visually Constructed (VC). The general rule is that when new visual information is being constructed, the eyes go automatically up to the left. This eye position can be observed in everyday life when a person is asked a specific question about constructing new visual information, e.g. designing a new home, dress or garden.

This rule for the general population, who are predominantly right dominant i.e. right handed, is twofold: if known information is being accessed the eyes go up to the right, and when new information is being accessed, the eyes go up to the left.

Picture: *Example of eyes positioned up to the left to visually construct new information*

Watch How the Eyes Access the Visual Memory

You may like to observe people's eyes and notice if they move up to the left, usually for a brief moment, if you ask questions about constructing, creating or designing something like a new craft project. As people have been told that it is polite to look directly at a person when speaking, their eyes may look straight at you, however, once relaxed, their eyes should move automatically upwards to the left to access and start constructing a picture in the visual memory. This is the general rule for right handed persons, but there are exceptions, such as for the left handed person, whose eyes could move up to the right.

My approach is to primarily use the Visually Constructed method to directly access the visual memory to imprint and lock new spelling words into short and long term memory. This knowledge has revolutionised the visualisation process, and when implemented through the S.P.E.L.L Method, in only 5 minutes a day each week, a few new words can be learned easily and with high accuracy.

New words are stored accurately in the visual memory by simply moving both eyes upwards and to the left, about the height of the forehead, to look at the words. This position imprints new spelling directly and accurately into the visual memory for storage into long term memory. As the visual memory is located in the brain across the back of the head, the old adage, *"I can see you with the eyes at the back of my head"* is literally quite true. The visual memory is similar to the storage capacities of a memory chip in a camera, or the hard drive of a computer. Although the eyes are linked directly to the visual memory, they can be likened to the lens of a camera as they take only pictures or images of the world around us.

Typical Sample of a Child's Work

Before starting the S.P.E.L.L Method, selected words are tested to identify which words need to be learned. This is a typical example of children's misspellings.

Example 1: Omission of double letters
      e.g. *begining* for beginning,
      biger for bigger

Example 2: Generalisations
      e.g *beleave* for believe
      could for called

Example 3: Omission of letters
      e.g. *chistmas* for Christmas

Example 4: Substitutions
      e.g. *clen* for clean

Example 5: Insertions
      e.g. *Chothes* for clothes

Example 6: Spelling as it sounds
      e.g. *cantry* – country

Sample: *Example of commonly misspelt words*

If words are misspelt, they need to be learned again to imprint them correctly into the visual memory. Time and time again, words are often reproduced inaccurately as in these examples of misspelt words.

How to Imprint New Words Accurately into the Visual Memory

Let's look at the basic steps needed to access the visual memory and learn new words. The example given is the spelling of the word *there*.

Step 1   POSITION - Eyes Up to the Left

Move both eyes upwards and to the left, about the height of the forehead, to look at unfamiliar words, written on paper, in colours and lower case.

Position Eyes Up to the Left.

Turn eyes up to the left at forehead level to imprint *t-h-e-r-e* directly into the visual memory.

Step 2   ENTER - Learn New Word Silently

Enter each new word into the visual memory by silently visualising it internally, first forwards and then backwards. By listening to the inner verbalisation of a word, there is an automatic checking process that identifies any mistake. When this process is first learned, several or more rehearsals may be needed to memorise the correct letter order. Usually it takes about 10-15 seconds per word.

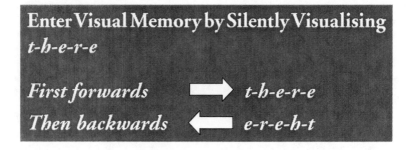

Enter Visual Memory by Silently Visualising *t-h-e-r-e*

First forwards   ➡️   *t-h-e-r-e*

Then backwards   ⬅️   *e-r-e-h-t*

Step 3   LISTEN as Each Word is Spelt Aloud

Spell the new word aloud, first forwards and then backwards, until accuracy is achieved. This may take several attempts. Once a word is spelt accurately backwards, it is usually imprinted into both the visual and long term memory.

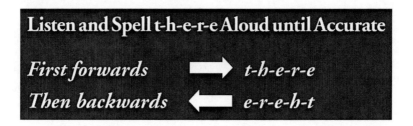

Listen and Spell t-h-e-r-e Aloud until Accurate

First forwards   ➡️   *t-h-e-r-e*

Then backwards   ⬅️   *e-r-e-h-t*

Step 4   REPEAT Until Correct

Repeat steps 1-3 until a word is accurately spelt, both forwards and backwards (note that correct spelling backwards is critical for accurate imprinting into the visual memory and then retention into long term memory).

> ## Repeat Steps 1-3 until *t-h-e-r-e* is Imprinted into the Visual Memory.

Improving Spelling Accuracy

Practise this simple technique for just 5 minutes a day to accelerate the accurate and speedy learning of new words. Once this visualisation process is mastered, confidence increases, and the number and difficulty of words learnt each week will gradually increase.

Recommendation

Initially commence with four new words each week, at first selecting only entry level spelling. Once weekly success and increased confidence are established, increase the word number and level of difficulty.

CHAPTER 3

*Connect motions with concepts and the body
becomes a literal extension of the brain.*
Ben Johnson

How Movement Increases Learning

Through natural movement, the foundations of learning are established and integrated within the first seven years of life. As part of this process, and to reach one's physical, emotional and intellectual potential, accurate processing of incoming information from the senses must be achieved.

Ayres (1994, p. 27) states the essential outcomes of this process are "awareness, perception, and knowledge, and ... the planning and coordination of movements, emotions, thoughts, memories and learning." Ayres also says that "the brain must organise all of these sensations if a person is to move and learn and behave normally" (ibid p. 5). The importance of the connection between the brain and the body is reiterated by Goddard (2009, p. 41) who states that "all learning takes place in the brain, but it is the body which acts as the vehicle by which knowledge is acquired. Both brain and body work together through the central nervous system."

The importance of the senses is outlined by Steiner (1966, p. 120) who says that the first four basic senses that we have are the "sense of touch, sense of life, of movement and of balance." These lay the foundations for learning. The importance of integrating sensory information is also emphasised by Goddard's statement (2009, p. 24) that "nothing that is seen is understood by the sense of vision alone... what we experience through vision as adults is actually the product of years of *multi*sensory experience... which has developed as a result of sight combined with moving, touching..."

However, sometimes developmental stages are incomplete as various causes hamper the processing of sensory information. Learning becomes a struggle. Some common indicators are: low academic achievement; an inability to sit still; poor concentration; inappropriate social interactions; poor memory; awkwardness or clumsiness; reading/maths at below age level; constant chatter; inability to interpret instructions accurately; fidgeting; disorganisation; restless sleep; and behaviours ranging from naughtiness to being withdrawn.

If a child is not responding to the S.P.E.L.L. Method, there could be underlying causes that need to be addressed and assessed by a therapist so that a program of specific movement patterns can be developed to assist integrating information from the senses, to increase academic potential. Because of my knowledge of specific movements that assist learning, the S.P.E.L.L. Method includes some fundamental movement patterns that may increase spelling success by removing or reducing some blocks to learning.

Let's look at a few underlying reasons why some children struggle to learn, and discover how simple, innate movement patterns can increase their learning potential.

1. Crossing the Midlines

Midlines are invisible lines that separate the body into the three different midlines or planes, which can be referred to as the front and back midline or Frontal Plane, the above and below midline or Horizontal

Plane, and the left/right midline or Sagittal Plane (McAllen, 2002). During the first seven years, crossing the midlines of the body is an important prerequisite to build learning pathways in the brain for the normal development of various gross and fine motor skills and academic learning. The following outlines midline characteristics, and how they can affect the developmental stages when midlines have not been crossed.

a) **Back and Front Midline (Frontal Plane)**

This 'midline' that develops from birth - 2.5 years, is an imaginary line drawn along the side of the body to separate the front of the body from the back. It starts at the top of the head and goes down to the soles of the feet. Ideally, both sides of the body work together smoothly and simultaneously. Competent gross motor skills will be the expected outcome. The inability to cross this midline affects basic gross motor skills, language development and fine motor skills.

b) **Above and Below Midline (Horizontal Plane)**

This 'midline' that develops between 2.5 - 4 years, is an imaginary horizontal line that is drawn at waist level and separates the upper body from the lower body. The horizontal midline is crossed by bending over from the waist.

Note that by four as the horizontal midline is developing, there is also the beginning of laterality which means the specialisation of the hemispheres of the brain, as the right side of the body can perform different skills to the left side of the body. Examples of specialisation at this stage include the commencement of using the dominant hand to write, draw, cut with scissors and throw a ball; an awareness of left and right; eyes and hands crossing the midlines; and skills such as riding a tricycle. Note that the language centre should be establishing itself in the dominant left hemisphere of the brain. Ambidexterity, the use of both sides of the body, is natural at this stage and includes "movement, hearing (hearing words), sight (seeing words) and speech (speaking words)..." (McAllen 2004, p. 6). It usually lasts till a child is five or six years old. One sided body skills that are developed include holding and kicking a ball, overhand throwing, and hopping.

c) **Left and Right Midline (Sagittal Plane)**

The vertical midline that develops between 5 - 8 years is outlined by McAllen (1998, p. 71) as an "invisible vertical 'wall' through the centre of the body that divides the body into left and right halves. It is present in a young child to enable both sides to develop... This barrier should have disappeared by the age of seven." At this stage of development, the left and right hemispheres of the brain begin to work together and information passes across the corpus callosum more efficiently. Because both sides of the body can now operate differently and independently from each other, cross lateral movement patterns become co-ordinated and instinctive, as opposite and different sides of the body cross over at the same time to complete an activity, e.g. left hand touches right leg, and then right hand touches left leg. The inability to cross this midline affects dominance, reading, writing and drawing and cross lateral patterns. Of particular relevance for learning are the following problems:

- **Writing and Drawing**

  When there is an inability to cross this 'midline' comfortably, writing and drawing can be limited to one side of the paper that is closest to the writing hand, or the pencil is switched from one hand to the other, or the book can be placed on one side of the desk to avoid crossing the midline.

- **Reading**

  For good reading to occur, both eyes need to team together efficiently, usually around 7 - 8 years of age, and cross the midline. The dominant eye leads by tracking words across a page whilst the non-dominant eye imitates the exact movements and blends the information. Difficulties crossing the vertical midline can cause poor reading as the "student may blink involuntarily... the eyes may also jerk with a very fine, subtle movement and/or they may lose the object they are tracking just as it reaches this midline" (McAllen 1998, p. 71). This causes the rereading of lines, skipping lines, loss of reading place, or omission of words.

- **Cross Lateral Patterns**

    When these patterns are not developed, movement patterns are limited to one side of the body, e.g. the left hand touches the left knee and right hand touches right knee. Many early year rhymes and rhythms assist with the development of one-sided movement and progress to cross lateral patterns, e.g. Pease Porridge Hot, Pease Porridge Cold, and The Sailor went to Sea, Sea, Sea. (For similar games refer to *Games Children Play: How Games and Sport Help Children Develop* Brooking Payne 1994)

2. Establishing Dominance

Dominance is the establishment of the use of only one side of the body to carry out various daily tasks. The right side of the body is the usual side for dominance to develop, e.g. right hand for writing, right foot for kicking balls, right eye to lead the left eye when reading, and the right ear for listening. Dominance is usually fully established between six to seven years.

When dominance is well established, specific areas of the brain have specific roles in processing information. The process is twofold. Information received from the right side of the body (e.g. right eye, arm, leg and ear) is processed in the left hemisphere, and information from the left side of the body (e.g. left eye, arm, leg and ear) is processed in the right hemisphere. This specialisation process is known as lateralisation and its importance is clearly explained by Ayres (1994, p. 33) who points out that "good lateralisation is probably the end product of normal brain growth and maturation."

Picture: *Example of dominance - right hand*

When dominance or lateralisation is not established, the brain receives mixed messages from different sides of the body and this causes inaccurate processing of sensory information. Here are two examples of how specialisation can occur in either or both of the left and right hemispheres of the brain, depending on which side of the body dominance has developed.

i. **Language**

For the right handed person, language functions such as grammar, vocabulary and meaning, as well as language production, are lateralised in the left hemisphere of the brain. Blomberg & Dempsey (2011, p. 149) have written that, "96% of all right handed people have their speech centre in the left hemisphere." For the left handed person, the lateralisation process is as variable as 70% have the dominant speech centre in the left hemisphere, 15% in the right hemisphere, and the remaining 15% have no preferences as both hemispheres are equally dominant.

ii. **Hearing**

The work of Dr. Tomatis, ENT specialist and a pioneer of sound therapy, is outlined by Goddard (1996). The best ear to process sound accurately is the right, as it directly accesses the main language centre which is located in the left hemisphere of the brain.

When sound is first heard with the left ear, information can sometimes be lost or misheard as there is a gap in the processing procedure, as information needs to be transferred from the right hemisphere to the left hemisphere. Examples of misinterpreted auditory information:

Example 1:
Words that are heard with the left ear arrive a bit later than words heard with the right ear, e.g. the word *um-brel-la* can be heard as *um-la-brel*.

Example 2:
When words are heard with the left ear, often only two out of three instructions are remembered as the third one would have been lost in the process of transferring the first two pieces of information from the right hemisphere to the left hemisphere.

3. Developing Spatial Orientation

The balance system needs to be functioning properly for spatial orientation as well as keeping an upright posture. These outcomes are achieved from interpreting information from the muscles and joints, eyes, and the inner ear's three semicircular canals, the vestibular.

Balance is developed during the formative years. "It is the first system to be fully developed, becoming operational at 18 weeks in utero" states Goddard (1996, p. 42). From movements in utero and exploratory limb movements of a baby whilst lying on her back, to rolling over and rising up to commence crawling, and then standing up and walking in all directions - all stem from the balance mechanism of the ear.

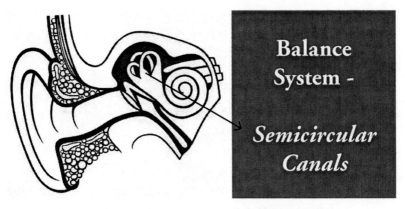

Diagram: Inner ear's semicircular canals

The balance system is connected to the three midlines (the vertical - left/right, horizontal- above/below, and the frontal - front/back) as each corresponding semicircular canal is linked to a "motion in different planes in space" (Goddard Blythe 2004, p. 14). Spinning and turning are linked to the *vertical midline*; movements that go up and down like seesaws are linked to the *horizontal midline*; moving both forwards or backwards like rocking, nodding, swinging, hanging and swaying are linked to the *frontal midline*.

The importance of the balance system is reiterated by Ayres (1994, p. 37) who states that the "vestibular system is the unifying system" and that "vestibular input seems to 'prime' the entire nervous system to function effectively." When the balance system is not operating effectively "the interpretation of other sensations will be inconsistent and inaccurate, and the nervous system will have trouble getting started" (ibid p. 37).

When the balance system is not well developed, there can be many areas that are affected:

   i.   Movements can be unsteady causing falls, stumbling, tripping or knocking into things.

   ii. Vision can be blurry from movements of the head, the sun's glare and poor eye-hand co-ordination.

iii. The hearing of sounds may be muffled, especially in noisy environments, and there may be the occurrence of ear aches and motion sickness.

Improve Learning with Simple and Effective Movement Patterns

Very simple, rhythmic and natural movement patterns that cross midlines, develop touch and balance, align dominance, and improve spatial orientation, have been included in the S.P.E.L.L. Method. Learning success is increased when rhythm is included in the learning process. Rhythms are noticed in our physical movements, waking and sleeping, speech production, emotions and thoughts as well as in subconscious rhythms of the heartbeat and breath. Rhythm is a fundamental function in the learning of spelling.

Each new movement pattern needs to be demonstrated by a teacher to ensure accuracy and imprinting into the brain stem. (Refer Section 2, Chapter 4) Each week spelling should improve, if after learning new words using Steps 1-4 of the S.P.E.L.L. Method, they are consolidated by rehearsing them again in Step 5, using rhythmic movement patterns in synchronicity with each syllable. The following two steps are most important and this sequence must be repeated until the words are spelt correctly with movement patterns.

1. Visualise the word again with the eyes looking up to the left, and silently spell the word both forwards and backwards. (Step 3 – E for Enter)

2. **Without looking at the word, spell it aloud both forwards and backwards whilst moving in time with the selected movement pattern and rhythm of each word**. (Step 4 - L for Listen and Step 5 – L for Let's Move)

From my experience, I have found that when movement is added to the visual memory process, spelling accuracy may be initially reduced, but by repeating these two steps until there is correct spelling, new words are firmly imprinted into the visual memory. The following movement patterns are easy to do either at home, or in the classroom.

a. Very Simple Rhythmic Movements

Purpose

This movement stimulates and integrates:

- front and back midlines (Frontal Plane)
- visual area in the front space and the hearing area in the back space

Directions

- **Rocking Forwards and Backwards**
  Alternate body weight rhythmically from the front foot to the back foot.

- **Walking Forwards and Backwards**
  Walk both forwards and backwards in rhythm with each syllable.

Picture: Example of Rocking Forwards and Backwards

b. Simple Spatial Orientation and Midline Movements

Purpose

These simple movement patterns stimulate spatial orientation awareness, or sense of space around the body, and cross and integrate the three midlines or planes. The following two exercises have been adapted from *Take Time: Movement Exercises for parents, teachers and therapists of children with difficulties in speaking, reading, writing and spelling* (Nash-Wortham & Hunt 2003, The Robinswood Press, England).

Circular movement around the vertical line through the body defines the surrounding peripheral space and integrates the three midlines.

Directions

Circular Movement Whilst Standing

1. Extend both arms down the sides of the body at upper thigh height level.
2. Hold the bean bag in the right or dominant hand. Pass it to the left hand.
3. Move both hands around to the back of the body at the same time, and pass the bean bag from the left hand to the right hand.
4. Move both hands back to the centre.
5. Continue the circular pattern.
6. Extend movement by moving forwards and backwards.

Picture: *Example of Circular Movement Whilst Standing*

(My observations are that when a word is spelt backwards, the circular movement changes directions)

c. Cross-Lateral Activities

Purpose

Cross lateral movements stimulate the left and right hemispheres of the brain (Dennison & Dennison 1989) and integrate the above/below and left/right midlines.

Directions

- ## Opposite Shoulders and Hands

  Touch the opposite shoulder with the opposite hand. Right hand touches left shoulder and alternates with left hand to touch right shoulder. Continue pattern.

Picture: Example of Opposite Shoulders and Hands

- ## Opposite Elbows and Hands
  Touch the opposite elbow with the opposite hand. Right hand touches the left elbow and is alternated with left hand touching the right elbow. Continue pattern.

Picture: Example of Opposite Elbows and Hands

- ## Opposite Knees and Hands
  Touch the opposite knee with the opposite hand. Right hand to left knee alternates with left hand to right knee. Continue pattern.

Picture: Example of Opposite Knees and Hands

Extension of Exercises

When competence is gained with the new movement exercises, moving both forwards and backwards can be included in the learning process.

Conclusion

Rhythmic movement patterns are the last step of the S.P.E.L.L Method. Words are both visualised silently and then spelt out aloud both forwards and backwards whilst moving rhythmically to specific movement patterns and language structures. This is an integral part of the learning process.

CHAPTER 4

The brain must organise all of our sensations if a person is to move and learn and behave in a productive manner.

Dr A J Ayres

What the Brain Can Do and More!

Introduction

By understanding the brain's developmental stages and their functions we can accelerate the learning processes, both for spelling and general educational applications.

The brain houses and transmits all sensory information; its phenomenal growth in the first seven years builds the foundations for learning and life. Each stage has its specific sequential task and needs to be supported by healthy, natural educational activities. Only when the brain is functioning effectively as a whole, are body movements co-ordinated and learning enhanced. When the brain is not accurately processing information from the senses, then learning becomes a struggle, body movements are clumsy, social skills are poor, and academic achievements are low.

Brain Structures

One useful model of the sequential stages of the brain was developed by Paul MacLean, Chief of the Laboratory of Brain Evolution and Behaviour at the National Institute of Mental Health in Bethesda Maryland, who in 1952 coined the *Triune Brain* model (Brewer & Campbell 1992, p. 198). MacLean identifies three basic components: the brain stem or reptilian brain; the emotional brain, which he calls the mid brain or limbic system; and, the outer layer of the brain or the intelligent section, which he calls the Neocortex.

These three areas have specific, highly specialised functions to accurately process all sensory information for one's wellbeing and potential. They are:

1. **Brain Stem** (stimulus response and basic survival)
2. **Emotional Brain/Limbic System** (emotional and memory centre)
3. **Intelligent Brain** (outer layer that controls higher levels of thinking through the cerebral cortices and the Neocortex)

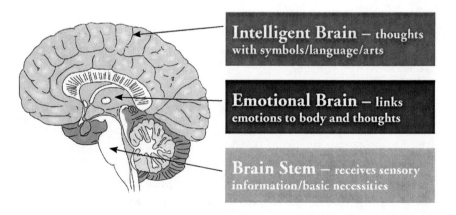

Intelligent Brain – thoughts with symbols/language/arts

Emotional Brain – links emotions to body and thoughts

Brain Stem – receives sensory information/basic necessities

Diagram: Triune Brain

1. Brain Stem

- **Development Time**

This develops between conception and fifteen months.

- **Characteristics**

The brain stem is the oldest part of the brain and is located about the height of the ears. It oversees basic necessities such as food, sleep and alertness to danger or stress. Nerve nets must first develop here for all sensory information to be received, interpreted and transmitted automatically and accurately before higher functions of the brain can operate. Behind the brain stem sits the cerebellum, often called the little brain as it contains over 50% of the total number of neurons in the brain. Its many functions include the maintenance of balance, timing and pressure for body movements, and certain cognitive functions such as language.

- **Educational Activities**

Free play and unrestrained exploration in a safe environment are essential for the healthy growth of the neurons in the brain. A baby discovers its environment and develops a sense of space through free movements such as waving its limbs; lifting the body; rolling over and raising the head; rocking, crawling and finally walking. Unfortunately a baby's innate movement patterns are often restricted through apparatuses such as bouncinettes, rockers, and play pens – all of which should be avoided.

Throughout early childhood, the continual development of gross motor skills, e.g. rolling, climbing, running, swinging and skipping, stimulate these nerve nets in the brain to form the foundations for higher learning. Blocks to learning can often occur here, and they can be removed or reduced through various movement patterns. (Refer Section 2, Chapter 3)

- **S.P.E.L.L Method**

Some basic and simple movement patterns that stimulate new neural networks in the brain stem and cerebellum are included in the S.P.E.L.L Method.

2. Emotional Brain (Limbic System)

- **Development Time**

This develops between 15 months to 4½ years.

- **Characteristics**

The emotional brain or limbic system intricately links body, thoughts and emotions so they function as a whole. Although thoughts develop in the intelligent part of the brain, they are directly connected with emotions and cognitive processes. By 15 months of age, the emotions are first linked to sensory input and learned motor functions and are then stored in short term memory, and finally into long term memory to make sense of the world and for learning.

Enriching emotions at this stage is essential for the individual's ability to understand relationships, and to develop rational thought, imagination, creativity and a healthy body. The utmost importance of imagination for learning was stressed by Albert Einstein (cited in Hannaford 1995, p. 63) who states that "imagination is more important than knowledge, for while knowledge points to all there is, imagination points to all there will be." He believed that play is the highest form of research. Paul MacLean (Brewer & Campbell 1992) also emphasises that the imagination and high level reasoning develop through creative play.

- **Educational Activities**

  Through free creative play, the imagination becomes engaged, especially when the child plays with natural materials like sand, or natural objects such as shells, sticks or stones, and uses these items as imaginary toys in an ever flowing stream of creativity. Reading and retelling stories also allows both younger and older children to expand their imagination.

- **S.P.E.L.L Method**

  New words can be made interesting and different if learnt by association through creating imaginative stories which activate both short term and long term memory. Stories often present themselves by simply looking at the structure of a word. Drawing a picture/s about the story further aids recall into long term memory.

Example 1: *sandcastle*
The words within the word are ***sand*** and ***castle***. A simple story could be **"With *sand*, the children built a *castle* at the beach."** A picture of a sandcastle triggers associations between the words *sand* and *castle*.

Example 2: *some*
Some can become two words - *so* and *me*. A memorable and funny story could be **"*So* what about *me* and my cat coming to your party?** A picture of a cat triggers an association with the word ***some.***

3. Intelligent Brain

a. Cerebrum

Development Time

Components of the cerebrum, "the occipital, temporal and parietal areas partially develop along with the brain stem and limbic systems but exhibit a major growth spurt at approximately age four. It is not until approximately age eight that we get a major growth spurt in the frontal lobes" Hannaford (1995, p. 76).

- **Characteristics**

    The cerebrum is the largest part of the brain and has four major divisions: frontal, parietal, temporal and occipital lobes. It also has two hemispheres, the right and left. "All of these lobes accept external stimuli and information from the opposite side of the body, via the brain stem and limbic system" (Hannaford 1995, p. 75). Each lobe has a clear function as outlined below and spelling tasks involve each lobe.

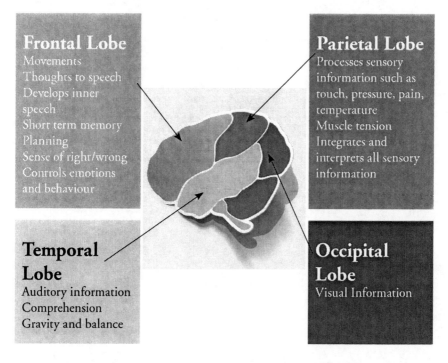

Frontal Lobe
Movements
Thoughts to speech
Develops inner speech
Short term memory
Planning
Sense of right/wrong
Controls emotions and behaviour

Parietal Lobe
Processes sensory information such as touch, pressure, pain, temperature
Muscle tension
Integrates and interprets all sensory information

Temporal Lobe
Auditory information
Comprehension
Gravity and balance

Occipital Lobe
Visual Information

Diagram: *Four lobes in cerebrum*

i. Occipital Lobe

The occipital lobe lies across the back of the brain and links the left and right hemispheres of the brain to process visual information. This visual information processing is enormously complex because it involves the three lobes of the cortex, the "occipital, temporal and parietal," to make sense of what is seen (Zillmer & Spiers 2001, p. 125).

The use of the occipital lobe is a key factor in the S.P.E.L.L. Method.

*   **S.P.E.L.L Method**

    The method allows the student to memorise patterns and shapes correctly each time, and to gradually develop a sense that a misspelt word just doesn't look right, so the visual memory is accessed again to identify the correct pattern and shape.

ii. Temporal Lobe

The temporal lobe (ears or sides of brain) processes auditory information such as sound, pitch and rhythm, comprehends language and provides a sense of gravity and balance. These are directly linked to the memory centres of the limbic system such as long term memory.

*   **S.P.E.L.L Method**

    Distinct, clear and precise articulation by the teacher increases the child's ability to hear accurately the various syllables and letter combinations in sentences. It also gives a student an excellent model to hear and reproduce sounds and syllables correctly. Sound combinations can be often misheard, such as the following examples.

    *Example 1: **th** can be misheard as **f***
    *Example 2: **b** can be misheard as either **v** or **d** or **p** or **w***

iii. Frontal Lobe

The frontal lobe (front of brain) processes and controls voluntary movements all over the body and develops skilled movements, translates thoughts into speech and develops inner speech, oversees short term memory tasks, planning, motivation, sense of right/wrong, and emotional and behaviour control.

- **S.P.E.L.L Method**

   Clear enunciation of each spelling word by the teacher ensures that its meaning and its structure can be understood and processed accurately by the learner. Putting each word in a sentence further helps the student to correctly assess its meaning. Both these strategies ensure accurate transferral of new words into long term memory.

iv. Parietal Lobe

The parietal lobe (top of brain) processes sensory information such as touch, pressure, pain, temperature, and muscle tension and integrates and interprets all sensations.

- **S.P.E.L.L Method**

   When a word is written down it assists spelling as the eyes automatically trace the direction and formation of each letter to imprint the pattern into the visual memory. Tactile experiences such as tracing words on the back of one's hand, further connects letter patterns to the visual memory.

b. Neocortex - Left and Right Hemispheres of the Brain

Development Time

The intelligent brain develops in the following sequential order.

Right Hemisphere 4.5 - 7 years   **Left Hemisphere** 7 - 9 years

- **Characteristics**

Sperry and Ornstein received a Nobel Prize for their discovery that there are two hemispheres of the brain, the left and right, "connected by an incredibly complex network of up to 300 million nerve fibres called the Corpus Callosum" (Rose 1985, p. 11). They also noted that the two halves had different functions.

The two cerebral hemispheres represent the "most recently evolved brain structure in humans" (Zillmer & Spiers 2001, p. 100) and its complexity "allows humans to use abstract concepts such as symbols, language and art."

The right hemisphere is associated primarily with images, meaning through context, appreciation of music and rhythmic patterns, day dreaming and intuition. The left hemisphere is associated primarily with language, detail and sequences, step by step strategies and finally analysis. The following diagram outlines the basic characteristics of each side of the brain.

Right Hemisphere		**Left Hemisphere**
Imagination/Patterns	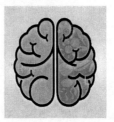	*Language*
Context		*Detail*
Colour		*Sequence*
Rhythms and Music		*Step by Step*
Intuition		*Analysis*
Development	**Corpus Callosum**	**Development**
4½ - 7 years.	Nerve nets connecting both hemispheres of the brain	7 - 9 years

From understanding the specific functions and characteristics of the left and right hemispheres, spelling progress can be accelerated.

Overview of S.P.E.L.L Method for
Right and Left Hemispheres

This diagram gives an overview of the roles of the right and left hemispheres in learning to spell *house.*

<u>*Right Hemisphere*</u>   <u>Left Hemisphere</u>

House

Images/ **Patterns**	*Visualisation, Lower case*	**Language**	*Recognises word, articulation*
Context	*Meaning*	**Detail**	*Accuracy*
Colour	*Images, Association*	**Sequence**	*Correct sequence*
Rhythms and Music	*Rhythms, Music*	**Step by Step**	*Practice steps*
Intuition	*Feeling - sense of right/wrong spelling*	**Analysis**	*Identifying correct letter patterns*

When the right hemisphere of the brain hears the word *house,* it creates a picture or image of a house, seeks meaning, senses rhythm, creates associations, and is either developing or has developed a sense of whether the word is spelt correctly or incorrectly. When the left hemisphere hears the word *house,* the processes of analysis, accuracy, correct letter order and patterns are initiated to learn new words accurately.

Conclusion

Knowing these functions of the brain, helps us understand the learning process so that we can work with the brain's patterning to master new knowledge. The S.P.E.L.L. Method does this by tapping into each specific area of the brain to maximise learning.

CHAPTER 5

I never teach my pupils, I only provide the
conditions in which they can learn.
Albert Einstein

Visualisation Research and Its Importance

A block that can stop spelling success is ignorance of the importance of visualisation or visual imagery as a key factor in successfully learning spelling. This chapter will summarise the work of leading educational researchers on this subject.

1. Educational Use of Visualisation - Look and Learn

Visualisation as an important element in learning spelling reached greater prominence during the 1970s and 1980s with the adoption of the holistic language method. This method has a multisensory approach as its learning modes include the visual, auditory and kinaesthetic with the emphasis on visualisation. Many educationalists have extended the original *Look, Cover, Write, and Check* Method, first initiated by Arvidson in 1963 (Peters 1985), which still is a process continued in many Australian schools. The original method had just four steps:

1.   Look at the new word so that word patterns are seen clearly.

2. Cover the word so that it cannot be seen.
3. Write the new word from memory, saying it softly to yourself as it is being written.
4. Check that the new word is spelt correctly. If the new word is not spelt correctly, restart from the first step. Repeat process until the word is learned.

Other educationalists have developed this method as outlined by Westward (2014) to include the Look-Trace-Copy-Recall; *Say*-Cover-Write-Check; Cover-Copy-Compare; Look-Say-*Name*-Cover-Write-Check and Spelling with Imagery. It is agreed by various educators that "no-one would deny that spelling depends to a large degree on the visual memory but also that visual memory is not the only key" (ibid p. 3). Westward also emphasises that these methods are "actually multisensory in that it involves seeing the word, saying and hearing the word, and writing the word" (ibid p. 3).

2. Directly Accessing the Visual Memory

Bandler and Grinder, founders of Neurolinguistic Programming, identified a specific method for directly accessing the visual memory by turning the eyes up to the left to first visualise new words, and to then spell them accurately aloud both forwards and backwards. (Refer to Section 2, Chapter 2)

3. Comparing Visual Imagery and Other Strategies

Educationalist Margaret Peters outlines the importance of visual imagery in her book *Spelling: Caught or Taught? A New Look* (1985). She challenges two myths: spelling is not learned when reading as every single word or letter sequence is not consciously examined; and secondly, spelling is not picked up through listening. Her central theme that spelling is 'taught, not caught', draws on extensive research, outlining how good spellers examine words, notice differences in word structures and identify visual patterns. In brief, spellers learn to visualise words clearly.

Phonics

Quite early in the 20th Century, the question was asked: can spelling be taught primarily through phonics? Phonics is simply the system of relationships between letters and sounds in a language, e.g. knowing that the letter B has the sound of *b*. Educationalist Hilderbrandt (Peters 1985) suggests that when the emphasis is placed on phonics instead of time to visualise new words, phonics does not allow the eye to recognize whole patterns and their significant parts.

Spelling Rules

Research about the teaching of common spelling rules as a prime factor in learning spelling is challenged by Simon and Simon (1973) who emphasise that spelling will only be learned "if sufficient visual recognition of information is available..." (Peters 1985, p. 78). English spelling patterns vary considerably in the degree to which they follow rules. For example, the letter cluster *ough* is represented with the words *enough, though, through, cough, bough, bought,* and *hiccough,* and the pronunciation varies. However, there is a 75% consistency when rules are learned with specific structures.

Spelling through Reading

Later in the 20th century, Bryant and Bradley (Peters 1985) outlined that reading and spelling involve different learning processes since certain strategies that are engaged when reading are not used when spelling. This phenomena is explained by current research into the brain's specialised tasks. When reading, words are quickly scanned to gain the text's meaning. In this process, even when there are letters omitted or misused in a word/s, the reader can still make sense of the text. If the sentence is written incorrectly, e.g. 'the dxg baxxed' instead of 'the dog barked', the meaning is still gained by the reader. This strategy engages the right hemisphere of the brain which has the characteristic role of making meaning of the text, compared to the function of the left hemisphere of the brain which aims to recognise detailed structures and patterns in words.

That one doesn't learn to spell when reading is further supported by both Nisbet and Schonell. Nisbet (1941) indicates that when children read, they are only likely to learn "one new word out of twenty-five ..." (Peters 1985, p. 26), and that only 4 per cent of words read are likely to be spelt. However, if during the reading process, spelling words are closely examined, then there is an improvement in spelling. Schonell (ibid) supports the fact that the casual experience of words in reading time is insufficient to imprint them into the memory.

Spelling through Hearing

How important is hearing or listening in learning new spelling? Through a comparative study by Gates and Chase of the spelling abilities of deaf children and normal children with the same reading ability, "deaf children were found to be superior by three to four years" (Peters 1985, p. 28). The premise for this is that deaf children relied primarily on their visual patterns when they wrote words as they could not distinguish sound patterns through their auditory sense. The English language has many structural variables, as often different letter structures represent different sounds. One example is the interpretation of the consonant phonic *f* that can be written as either a *ph* as in *elephant* or *siphon*, or as *f* as in *fun, future, family*. Another example is the use of *a* as in *cat, hat, fat, matter* yet the pronunciation of *a* can change to another sound as in *was* and *what*. If children rely on their auditory sense alone they often spell '*what*' as '*wot*'. Other examples are homophones which are words that sound the same but have different structures, e.g. *where* and *wear*. In consequence, hearing is not a primary factor when learning spelling, as words can be written in many different ways that cannot be identified through sound alone.

Flash Cards

One early researcher, Hartman, (Peters 1985) emphasised the importance of the use of flash cards as they allow the whole word to be visualised by good spellers. He noted how visualisation processes were applied by good spellers, chiefly looking at the whole word, retaining it, and then examining the word to observe its specific characteristics.

In my early years of teaching new reading words in Years 1 and 2 in the 1970s, I often wondered how the children learned them. One method that I used was flashcards. The children sat on the floor and I would hold the cards up in front of them, saying each word and then let them carefully look at it to identify patterns and shapes. Little did I know that this upward position of their eyes correlated with the research findings of Bandler and Grinder (1979) re visual memory.

Just Looking at a Word

Another visualisation strategy was used by Higley and Higley (Peters 1985) whose method of teaching new words was to simply allow students time to really look at them, without saying, spelling or writing them, as these activities intruded upon the learning process. This early strategy is one part of the S.P.E.L.L Method that draws on Neurolinguistic Programming research.

Observing Eye Movements

The importance of eye movements scanning the structure and pattern of words was researched by Gilbert and Gilbert (Peters 1985). They observed the eye movement pattern of successful spellers, noting that there needs to be unlimited time for the structure of words to be fully examined by the eyes, which repeatedly move over the words. They concluded that "from looking at such eye movements it is known that good spellers make fewer and shorter fixations than poor spellers, see more of the word at a time, and make fewer regressive movements" (ibid p. 32).

Visual Memory Training

Radaker in 1963 researched the difference between one group that was trained over two weeks in utilising visual imagery in learning spelling, and another that was untrained. When the two groups were tested one year later the group trained in visual imagery scored significantly higher than the untrained group. Radaker stressed the importance of looking at the various visual characteristics of the structures of words. He emphasised that training in visual imagery "seems to be a very efficient way of exploiting our preferred senses..." to learn to spell (Peters 1985, p. 33).

4. Visualisation and Spelling Competence

Muriel Harris (1985), Professor of English and Director of the Writing Lab, Purdue University, outlines the inadequacy of current programs such as workbooks or reading programs, because most students are unwilling to invest the time needed, and she also rejects phonics as the major teaching method.

She supports the emphasis on auditory and visual strategies and quotes Shaughnessy's (Harris 1985, p. 2) perception about a misspeller's inattention to words on a page as a kind of "visual slurring". She, like Margaret Peters, quotes Gates and Chase (1926) on the superior spelling abilities of deaf children because of their necessity to visualise. Harris (ibid p. 4) specifically states that "weak spellers need assistance in seeing the specific errors that they are making." She believes in contrasting and highlighting the problem letter for it to be seen easily and in writing correct letters larger or darker than the others. Students need to identify error and categorise it. She would like to see "more and better developed methods which recognise the importance of visualisation in spelling proficiencies" (ibid p. 5).

5. Gifted Spellers and Visual Strategies

Logan, Olson and Lindsey (1987) in *Reading Psychology,* reported on strategies that were used by 98 highly gifted spelling finalists, in junior or middle school, who took part in the 1986 Scripps Howard National Spelling Bee in America. Open ended questions were asked about the spelling strategies the students used when learning to spell new or difficult words. Approximately half of the successful spellers used visual memory to form a mental picture of the word. Other successful strategies were linking the word to its dictionary meaning, then saying and writing the word. One key finding was that when encountering words that cannot be spelt phonetically, the most common strategy was to use visual memory.

6. Dyslexia and Visual Memory

A visual approach for spelling is outlined by Murphy (2004) in his book *Dyslexia: An Explanation.* Murphy believes that phonics only works well for phonetically based languages such as Spanish or Italian compared to non-phonetic languages such as English, because only half of its words are spelt phonetically. He also believes that after being taught phonetically, the brain automatically and naturally progresses to a visual process, and that we may have learned to spell in school using a phonetic strategy, but most of us have since abandoned it in favour of a visual strategy for learning words.

He writes that phonics is a useful starting point but is not necessarily suitable for all students, especially for some dyslexic students. He outlines current research carried out by Gabrieli and Klinberg at Stanford University where two groups of adults, with and without dyslexia, were given a standardised reading test whilst being scanned by DTI (Diffusion Tensor Imaging) which tracks the pathways of white matter in the brain to detect abnormalities. The results showed a difference between the two groups in the amount of myelination in the left hemisphere of the temporal and parietal lobes which are connected to the language centre of the brain. The results indicate a difference in speeds at which sound is transmitted along the nerve fibre between the two groups of adults. If the speeds are slow for dyslexics, then the processing of auditory information could affect the auditory learning style. His conclusion for teaching students with dyslexia is to use a visual approach that relies on long term visual memory, rather than short term auditory memory.

7. Visualisation and a Multisensory Approach

The article by Westwood (2014) "Spelling: do the eyes have it?" compares the various spelling methodologies proposed by many educators. Gabarro (ibid p. 3) notes that "good spellers recall a mental image of a new word when they think about how it is spelled" but whilst recognising the importance of visualisation other educators say visual imagery works best when it is paired with orthographic awareness, i.e. an awareness of "sound-to-letter correspondence" (ibid p. 3). Clear pronunciation by teachers, sounding words out aloud, and reading for immersion in language patterns - all these approaches help build phonemic awareness. There is also a recognition that by repeatedly tracing and writing words, particularly high frequency ones, can aid automatic recall, and that thinking processes that require the brain to spell, proof read, self correct and check for meaning are all aids in the spelling process. Westwood thus concludes that accurate spelling integrates vision, hearing, speech, writing and strategic thinking and he encourages teachers to adopt a multisensory approach that draws on a variety of strategies.

Conclusion

Educational research from all these sources thus reinforces the message that visual memory is an important factor in learning how to spell words. The S.P.E.L.L. Method specifically utilises Bandler and Grinder's method of directly accessing the visual memory by turning the eyes up to the left to both first visualise, and then spell new words accurately, both forwards and backwards.

The S.P.E.L.L. Method facilitates an integrative learning approach by drawing on the auditory modalities of hearing sounds and words through clearly articulated speech, and on the kinaesthetic modality by writing down words. It also further stimulates the visual memory by drawing on the latest research on brain functioning to use associations, emotion, colour and movement to stimulate the brain. Furthermore, the knowledge of language is developed during the process.

CHAPTER 6

If you can't explain it simply, you don't
understand it well enough.

Albert Einstein

What's Different to What I Do Now?

In the busy world of teaching with its very high demands, it is much easier to stay with the same method than change to a new one, yet spelling success is lessened when there is a limiting belief that current strategies are the only way. Using traditional strategies, often weak spellers need to spend more time learning by repetition, e.g. rewriting words many times, or completing spelling sheets of word families and rules. If poor spelling results remain the same, then there is frustration for both teacher and student.

With this book, educationalists and parents can now know why and how to implement the new S.P.E.L.L. Method to successfully teach spelling, and even tables, rather than continuing with current methods. To do this, the difference between current strategies and the S.P.E.L.L Method must be identified.

Comparison between Current Strategies and the S.P.E.L.L. Method

The following tables clearly outline the differences between current educational methods/strategies and the S.P.E.L.L. Method.

1. Visualisation Strategies

A specific method of visualisation is a key strategy for the S.P.E.L.L. Method.

Activity	Current Strategies	S.P.E.L.L. Method
1. Eyes look up to the left to directly access the visual memory.	No	Yes
2. Silently visualising words both forwards and backwards.	No	Yes
3. Spelling words aloud both forwards and backwards.	No	Yes
Total	0 /3	3/3

2. Writing Words

Writing words out is the first step to looking at a word.

Activity	Current Strategies	S.P.E.L.L. Method
1. Spelling book to record words.	Yes	Yes
2. Words initially written on A4 paper/booklet are displayed to practise visualisation technique.	No	Yes
3. Chunking of letters in groups for easy recall.	No	Yes
4. Words written in colours to highlight groups of letters.	No	Yes

	Current Strategies	S.P.E.L.L. Method
5. Difficult letters are written in red to access visual memory.	No	Yes
6. Difficult letters are highlighted in light yellow.	No	Yes
7. Words written in lower case.	Yes	Yes
8. Rewriting words to memorise.	Yes	No
9. Words displayed above eye level and to the left to be practised forwards and backwards from memory 5 minutes a night.	No	Yes
Total	3/9	8/9

3. Movement and Learning

Specific movement patterns increase learning by stimulating the brain.

Activity	Current Strategies	S.P.E.L.L. Method
1. Rhythmically move a bean bag from hand to hand whilst spelling the word from memory both forwards and backwards.	No	Yes
Total	0/1	1/1

4. Teaching Practices

A variety of teaching practices ensures interest and success.

Activity	Current Strategies	S.P.E.L.L. Method
1. Words learned through a multisensory approach.	Yes	Yes
2. Visualisation based on NLP research is the key method.	No	Yes

		Current Strategies	S.P.E.L.L. Method
3.	All activities match specific functions of the brain.	No	Yes
4.	Traditional methods are utilised, e.g. word families, spelling rules and phonics.	Yes	Yes
Total		2/4	4/4

5. Music and Learning

Research on how specific music relaxes the mind to increase learning is available.

Activity		Current Strategies	S.P.E.L.L. Method
1.	Classical Baroque music that relaxes the mind (e.g. Pachelbel's Canon in D major) is played whilst words or tables are being learnt.	No	Yes
Total		0/1	1/1

6. Homework Time

Practising words is a key to success.

Activity		Current Strategies	S.P.E.L.L. Method
1.	Short time frame of visualising words forward and backwards, 5 steps in 5 minutes each night, eliminates writing out words.	No	Yes
Total		0/1	1/1

Conclusion

The challenge of the S.P.E.L.L. Method is to recognise the underlying premise that spelling is primarily a visualisation process which integrates multisensory modalities. Current traditional practices could easily incorporate the S.P.E.L.L. Method into the first stage, *Look*, of the Look, Cover, Write, Check Method, or, it can be used simply as a strategy in its own right.

CHAPTER 7

I would teach children music, physics and philosophy;
but most importantly music, for the patterns in
music and all the arts are the keys to learning.

Plato

Music - One More Powerful Way to Learn

New educational practices can always be trialled and reviewed in tandem with the S.P.E.L.L. Method. One accelerated learning technique uses classical music to enhance learning. The founder was Dr. Georgi Lozanov, a leading Bulgarian research psychologist, who worked with his fellow researcher, Dr. Evelyna Gateva, to develop "a highly effective learning technique that uses Baroque music in a learning session she calls *passive concert reading*" (Brewer & Campbell 1992, p. 232). This system helps students to learn without trauma and stress.

Baroque music was written between 1600 and 1750 and is "characterised by a predictable rhythmic and harmonic structure" (Brewer & Campbell 1992, p. 232). Playing Mozart, according to French researcher Belange, "co-ordinates breathing, cardio-vascular rhythm and brain wave rhythm and leads to positive effects on health. It acts on the unconscious, stimulating receptivity and perception" (Rose 1985, p. 102).

It has the following characteristics and benefits:

- integrates inner speech and thought
- integrates left and right hemispheres of the brain
- gives a sense of stability because of the predictable nature of the music
- creates a calm mood
- slows body functions because the heart beat is the same as the music
- nourishes relaxed receptivity and perception in the subconscious mind

This method of playing appropriate music to enhance learning during a passive concert has been a useful tool to relax my clients whilst working with them and is outlined in the following steps.

Passive Concert Music

Specific pieces of Baroque music are played in the background to firstly relax the learner whilst new words are presented. Some suitable pieces of Baroque music to create a passive concert are the commonly used Pachelbel's Canon in D Major; Handel's Water Suite; Bach's Fantasy in G major or Fantasy in C Minor, and Mozart's Serenades, Violin Sonatas or String Quartets.

a) Relaxation Method

The learner relaxes with eyes closed, and listens to the gentle passive concert music for a short period of time whilst gently breathing in and out. The importance of relaxation and its effect on learning is emphasised by Wade (1990, p. 87) who notes that "although bodies are passive, minds are in hyper-drive."

b) Present One Word at a Time

After the learner is relaxed, present each new word individually to the rhythm of the music and in a natural way, as if the voice were an instrument in the orchestra.

- **Say and Spell the Word**

    Articulate each new word in a moderate tone that is a little softer than the background music.

- **Echo Time**

    Allow a silent space of a few seconds between each new word so that the brain can rehearse all the letters. The length of time depends on the length of the word.

    Example:

Pronunciation	Say	Echo Time or Pause
there	*t - h- e- r- e*	Echo Time 3-4 seconds
could	*c - o - u - l - d*	Echo Time 3-4 seconds
would	*w - o - u - l - d*	Echo Time 3-4 seconds

    The dash (-) symbol represents the slow pace of saying each letter.

Continue this pattern until all the words have been taught. Once finished, allow the learner to stretch gently and awaken from the relaxation state.

A passive concert can be pre-recorded for a learner to listen to during study sessions at home. Wade (1990 p. 69) says whilst the "passive concert is playing, relax and close the eyes and allow any multi-sensory sensations to come and go." Images appear and may be in many forms like colours, pictures or spelling patterns.

CHAPTER 8

The secret in education lies in respecting the student.
Ralph Waldo Emerson

Frequently Asked Questions

1. Can the S.P.E.L.L Method be Used in the Classroom?

The S.P.E.L.L Method has been specifically written to assist teachers in the classroom and parents who help their child/ren at home. Its simple visualisation techniques and methods work well even in restricted spaces and have been trialled in primary classrooms.

2. Can Spelling Problems be Resolved through Learning More Spelling Rules?

Children who struggle to learn have had teachers of a very high calibre teaching them spelling rules, phonics and word families, yet they still misspell words. By first directly accessing the visual memory, and integrating it with existing teaching, the accuracy of spelling increases.

3. What is the Effect of Movements on the Results?

Although good results can be achieved utilising only the visualisation technique, from my years of experience as a Threefold Therapist for Learning, I have found that students have always improved in learning, confidence and independence if simple movement patterns are also applied. These exercises, as outlined in Sections 1 and 2, have been adapted for both the classroom and home.

4. Can the S.P.E.L.L Method be Applied in Other Academic Areas?

I have also found that the S.P.E.L.L Method can be easily applied in other academic areas, such as learning multiplication tables, identifying new words from reading, and memorising mind maps.

5. Do Newly Learned Words Transfer to Writing?

There are a few stages in the primary classroom writing process in Australia. The first part of the process is a rough draft. Here, often words may be misspelt, even by competent spellers, as the content of the writing is the focus. Later in the drafting process, incorrect words are often identified and written out correctly as students have developed a sense that the word *doesn't look right.*

From my experience, students who have learned the S.P.E.L.L Method develop this sense that the word *doesn't look right* and with practice, they start to apply themselves to reread their written work to identify and correct misspelt words. The first step is for students to gain spelling confidence and then develop the new skill of proof reading their written work.

SECTION 3

Case Studies – From Underachievement to Success

(This section **proves** it works)

CHAPTER 9

Our greatest weakness lies in giving up.
The most certain way to succeed is always
to try just one more time.
Thomas A. Edison

Case Studies –
How Underachieving Students Succeeded

Introduction to Case Studies

The first section of this chapter reports on two longitudinal case studies which demonstrate the success of the S.P.E.L.L method. The second section focuses on two general case studies.

Longitudinal Case Studies

The first longitudinal case study took place over 6 terms at a Melbourne metropolitan primary school whose principal was looking for a new way to assist underachieving literacy students. It achieved an averaged success rate of 79%.

The second case study focuses on a Year 2 student who commenced the movement patterns program. Her spelling results were averaged both before and after the implementation of the S.P.E.L.L Method to show progress over 32 weeks. There was a 95% success rate. Results from the standardised South Australian Spelling Test were also collated to compare the difference between the expected age norm score and that achieved after the introduction of the S.P.E.L.L Method. There was an increase of 1.6 years in the student's spelling age norm.

General Case Studies

The second section collates results and work samples from two general case studies. The first case study gives samples of commonly misspelt words and shows how quickly new words can be retained into long term memory. The second case study shows how visualisation and classical Baroque music can assist the learning process.

A. Longitudinal Case Studies

Longitudinal Case Study 1 – Underachieving Primary Literacy Students

Overview

This case study took place at a Melbourne metropolitan school over 6 terms between 2001 and 2002. The subjects were twenty primary school students in the Years 3/4 Literacy Support Group Program who experienced great difficulties learning spelling. Each student was carefully selected to take part in the program, which utilised the S.P.E.L.L. Method plus movement patterns to reduce or remove blocks to learning in the central nervous system.

Methods Implemented

As the students experienced constant poor spelling results and had very low confidence in their academic abilities, it was decided that an individual 1:1 approach for weekly half hourly sessions would be the most beneficial. Four words were taught each week with the total number of words each term varying from 11–43 words depending on attendance, the number of weeks in each term and student ability. Words they needed to learn were taken from various literacy sources including their spelling folder, stories, and lists of commonly misspelt words that matched the students' current abilities.

It was decided that the approach be twofold to maximise results.

a. Movement Patterns

As each child had difficulties remembering spelling words, I presumed that there would be underlying learning difficulties. Using my expertise as a Threefold Therapy for Learning therapist, at the beginning of each session, for 5-10 minutes, I introduced simple movement patterns to reduce or remove retained reflexes that inhibit the learning processes in the higher functions of the brain. These movements were executed by most of the students.

b. S.P.E.L.L. Method

Refer Section 1.

Testing

At the beginning of each session, the previously taught spelling words were tested. At the end of each term, all words that had been taught were retested to assess retention in long term memory. Before this end of term testing, each child re-wrote all of the term's words and was asked to practise them at home for the test, usually held on the last week of term.

Data

To assess the group's progress, their spelling results were then collated and averaged over a period of 6 terms through two methods, which were firstly to calculate the total number of words correctly spelt and convert this into a term percentage, and secondly to average these term percentages.

1. **Percentage Calculated from Total Number of Correct Words Each Term**

    The percentage score was derived from the total number of correctly spelt words each term, and then divided by the total number of words tested each term.

    Example
    Term 2, 2001
    The number of correctly spelt words ÷ total number of words taught ×100
    213 ÷ 305 × 100 = 69.83% or 70% (converted to nearest decimal).

2. **Term Percentages Averaged Over 6 Terms**

    The percentages of each term were added together and then divided by the total number of terms which was 6.

    Example
    The terms' percentages were added together.
    70%+83%+ 80% +83% +83% + 76% = 475
    The average was calculated by dividing the total number of percentages by the number of terms which was 6.
    475 ÷ 6 = 79.16% or 79% (converted to nearest decimal)

Collation of Results

This graph represents the collated spelling results of 20 students over a period of 6 terms. Each term's percentage results were averaged. All these averages were then collated and a total average for the six terms was calculated.

Graph 1: Collated Percentages Over 6 Terms

Two conclusions can be drawn from this graph.

1. The averaged results varied between 70% and 83%.

2. **The averaged percentage over six terms was 79%.**

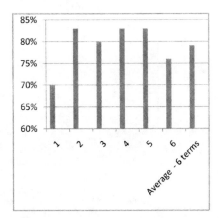

The following table represents the collation of all the terms' test scores of the twenty participating students, averaged as a percentage, and then averaged again as a percentage over six terms.

Table 1:
Each Student's Score Collated at the End of Each Term to Calculate Average Percentage Each Term, and Average Percentage Over 6 Terms

Student Scores and Percentages

Student Number	Year Level	Term 2 2001	Term 3 2001	Term 4 2001	Term 1 2002	Term 2 2002	Term 3 2002
		End of Term Scores	End of Term Scores	End of Term Scores	End of Term Scores	End of Term Scores	End of Term Scores
	4/5	14/27					12/21
	4	4/27	15/28				22/31
	3						15/22
	3						10/10
	3						9/15
	3/4						18/18
	4	17/30	26/38	17/33			
	3						18/18
	3/4	17/28	23/30	30/32			20/26
	4/5	13/13	36/39	27/36			
	4/5	27/27	24/28	22/34			
	3		38/38	37/42			
	4	13/25	26/26	27/28			
	3/4	16/18	20/25	28/37	40/42	24/25	
	3	31/31	23/28	32/35			
	3/4			17/18	32/41	26/33	10/16
	3	21/29	25/33	34/43			
	3/4	18/24	28/33	30/39	20/28	23/30	
	3						9/11
	3	22/26	30/34				
Total Number of Students Each Term		20	20	11	3	3	10
Total Number of Correct Words Each Term		213/305	314/380	301/380	92/111	73/88	143/188

Total Number of Correct Words Over 6 Terms	1136/1452					
Average Percentage Each Term	70%	83%	80%	83%	83%	76%
Average Percentage Over 6 Terms	**79% Success Rate**					

Conclusion

The tabled results have indicated a high level of retention of the words into long term memory. Over 6 terms there was a total number of 1452 words taught and a total of 1136 words retained in long term memory. This represents a 79% success rate.

On a more personal note, for one child, who struggled more than others, there is a story of triumph which I hope will encourage other students with weak results. He had hardly learnt any words at all, yet one day he achieved the seemingly impossible, a very high score. He was so pleased that he could not believe his eyes when he saw his mark. We returned to the classroom and he told the teacher his score. His teacher was so surprised and taken aback that the whole class became aware of her reaction. She told the class and they spontaneously started clapping. For that brief moment of achievement and pride, I hope he will treasure forever.

Longitudinal Case Study 2 - Underachieving Individual Student

Overview

The subject of this case study is an 8 year old female who in Year 2, 2013 was starting to fall behind academically. The teacher discussed with her parents the strong possibility that she would need to repeat

Year 2. After the implementation of the S.P.E.L.L Method, her spelling results over a period of 32 weeks indicated an immediate and significant success rate which averaged 95%.

This case study has two sections:

a. Collation of Results from Classroom Spelling Tests

This research records and compares the success rate in classroom spelling test scores of a Year 2 student which increased from 54% to 95% after the introduction of the S.P.E.L.L Method.

b. Comparison of Results of Standardised Spelling Tests

This research compares three assessments of the Standardised South Australian Spelling Test with the subject's scores indicating a marked increase in her spelling ability over a period of eight months. The student's first assessment indicated that she was 1.9 years below the norm for her chronological age, whereas by her third assessment her spelling age increased by 1.6 years and her score was 0.3 months below the norm for her chronological age.

Method

a. Movement and Learning Program

On the 16th March, 2013, the Movement and Learning Program was commenced to implement specific movement patterns that assist learning by removing or reducing blocks that cause inaccurate processing of sensory information in the brain.

b. S.P.E.L.L. Method

The visualisation process was learned halfway through the movement program on the 27th June, 2013, and was applied at home with the student practising the words 5 minutes nightly for

5-6 nights or 25-30 minutes each week. The words learned were from her classroom's new weekly or fortnightly spelling words.

Duration of Testing

The subject was tested weekly/fortnightly on her new spelling words in her classroom over a period of 8 months between March and November in 2013.

Collation of Results from Classroom Spelling Tests

At the end of each week's test of ten words, all the test results were recorded, collated and then averaged to compare results before and after the introduction of the S.P.E.L.L. Method.

1. **Monthly Averages of Correctly Spelt Words**

   Each week's score was totalled and averaged by the number of weeks in each month.
   Example
   March 4/10 + 3/10 + 5/10 + 5/10 = 17
   The average was calculated by dividing the total by the number of tests each month
   17 ÷ 4 = 4.25

2. **Monthly Averages of Correctly Spelt Words Before and After the S.P.E.L.L. Method**

   To compare the difference between the numbers of correctly spelt words before and after the implementation of the S.P.E.L.L. Method, each monthly average was added together and then divided by the number of months either before or after S.P.E.L.L. Method usage.

The following tables collate all test results between March and November in 2013.

Table 1: Comparison Average of Correctly Spelt Words Before and After the S.P.E.L.L. Method

Before S.P.E.L.L Method

Dates of Test Results & Scores out of 10					Number of Tests	Monthly Averages	Total of Monthly Average	Number Times 10/10 was achieved
March	1st	15th	22nd	28th	4			
	4/10	3/10	5/10	5/10		4.25		
April	6th	19th			2			
	5/10	9/10				7		0
May	3rd	17th	19th	24th	4			out
	6/10	6/10	7/10	6/10		6.25		of 14
June	7th	14th	21st	28th	4			tests
	6/10	4/10	5/10	2/10		4.25		
Totals					14	21.8	5.45	
Percentage Total of Monthly Averages							**54%**	

After S.P.E.L.L Method

						Number of Tests	Monthly Averages	Total of Monthly Average	Number Times 10/10 was achieved
July		19th	26th			2	10		
		10/10	10/10						
August	2nd	9th	16th	23rd	30th	5	8.75		
	10/10	8/10	9/10	8/10	10/10				13
September	2nd	6th	13th	20th	31st	5	9.75		out
	9/10	10/10	10/10	9/10	10/10				of 18
October		13th	18th	25th		3	10		tests
		10/10	10/10	10/10					
November		8th	15th	28th		3	9		
		8/10	10/10	9/10					
Totals						18	47.5	9.5	
Percentage Total of Monthly Averages								**95%**	

Analysis of Test Results

Clearly the S.P.E.L.L. Method has produced a dramatic improvement of 41% over 5 months for this student's monthly spelling averages.

Collation of Results from Standardised Spelling Test

Method

At each subsequent assessment, the subject's spelling ability was tested with the standardised South Australian Spelling Test (S.A.S.T), a graded list of 67 words for students between the ages of 6 and 16. This test was developed by Peters in 1970 to enable qualitative analysis of spelling errors for diagnostic purposes, especially for those in need of additional assistance in spelling. This table represents the results from three assessments of the standardised South Australian Spelling Tests.

Table 2: Table of Comparison of Results of Standardised Spelling Tests			
Standardised Test – South Australian Spelling Test.			
Assessment	1	2	3
Dates	28.2.2013	30.5.2013	31.10.2013
Movement Sessions	0	10 sessions	10 sessions
S.P.E.L.L Method Introduced for Homework	0	1 session Homework	Homework
Results	1.9 years below	1.4 years below	0.3 years below
Comparison of Assessment Results			
Assessments 1 & 2	*Increase 0.5 months*		
Assessments 2 & 3		*Increase 1.1 years*	
Assessments 1 & 3	*Increase 1.6 years*		

The student's spelling score was compared to that of students with the same chronological age. After the first assessment, her score was 1.9 years below the standard norm for her age group. After ten weekly 45 minute sessions with the Movement and Learning Program, her spelling result for Assessment 2 was now 1.4 years below the standard norm expected for her age group with an increase of 0.5 months since her first assessment. The S.P.E.L.L Method was introduced on the 27th June, 2013, and her spelling results for the second and third assessment increased by 1.1 years, only 3 months below the standard norm expected for her age group. The total increase in her spelling age between Assessment 1 and Assessment 3 was 1.6 years.

Conclusion

Results indicate a significant improvement in the student's spelling after the introduction of the S.P.E.L.L Method as 95% of test words were spelt correctly, and there was an increase of 1.6 years in the results of the standardised South Australian Spelling Tests.

B. Samples of General Case Studies

Subject 1: Common Spelling Problems

Overview

This case study indicates how weak spellers commonly misspell words and how quickly they can retain words into long term memory after commencing the S.P.E.L.L. Method. This subject was a Year 4 student who was greatly distressed at her weekly low spelling scores because her peers knew her results.

Method

a. Movement and Learning Program

On the 6.5.2012, the student commenced the Movement and Learning Program for movement patterns that remove or reduce inaccurate processing of sensory information that blocks learning. She completed twenty sessions.

b. S.P.E.L.L. Method

One month after starting the movement program, the S.P.E.L.L. Method was taught on the 6.6.2012 and the student learned new words from the classroom and practised them each night. Words were learnt in groups of four until she gained confidence with the new strategies.

Collation of Data

Below are two samples of the student's spelling tests. The first test (pre-test) demonstrates that she relied on the common strategy of sounding out words, or reproducing incorrect patterns from long term memory (to highlight the various spelling strategies she has used, her misspelt words have been categorised under headings beside the tests). The second test (post test) demonstrates that using the S.P.E.L.L. Method, 100% accuracy can be achieved in the classroom.

Sample 1: Collation of Data

Unit 29 Spelling Pretest	Spelling Post Test
1. *new* x (*knew*)	*knew*
2. *us* ʌ (*use*)	*use*
3. *afternoe* x (*afternoon*)	*afternoon*
4. ~~threw~~ *therw* x (*threw*)	*threw*
5. *Spone* x (*Spoon*)	*Spoon*
6. *rofe* x *roof*	*roof*
7. *qube* x (*cube*)	*cube*
8. *roall* x (*rule*)	*rule*
9. ~~hoouse~~ *house* x (*who's*)	*who's*
10. *fruite* x (*fruit*)	*fruit*
11. *hoouse* ʌ (*whose*)	*whose*
12. *threw* x (*through*)	*through*
13. *Tusday* x (*tuesday*)	*Tuesday*

Homophone confusion
- *who's* for whose
- *threw for* through

Silent letters
- *new for* knew

Patterns
- *spone for* spoon
- *afternoe for* afternoon

Omission of letters
- *Tusday for* Tuesday
- *us for* use:

Reversal of letters
- *therw* for threw
- *howse for* whose

Phonetic spelling
- *fruite for* fruit
- *rofe for* roof

Subject 2: Visualisation and Music

Overview

This is a case study of a Years 7/8 secondary student, a very poor speller, whose mother was very concerned that his academic progress would be overshadowed by this problem. By combining visualisation and classical Baroque music over five terms from 1995 to 1996 his spelling success was increased.

Method

a. S.P.E.L.L Method

All new words were taught with the S.P.E.L.L Method and each term's words were tested with the total number of words ranging between 50–125.

b. Classical Baroque Music

After the S.P.E.L.L Method practice, the student settled himself on the gym mat and pillow till he was comfortable and warm with a soft woollen blanket. Through a short progressive method of relaxation, his body relaxed and his mind quietened. Then he listened to each new word as I spoke them, at the same sound level as the specific classical piece, Pachelbel's Canon in D Major that was being played. Between each word, there was a pause of a few seconds, or for the length of time it took him to repeat the new word in his mind before the next word was presented. After all the words had been heard, he would gradually stir from this relaxed state ready to go home.

Results

Using this method, over three terms, the student's average test results varied from 85% to 94%. When he first started to visualise new words he found it difficult. After learning new words each week and practising them at home, he started visualising words more easily. He also attempted to spell difficult words that he wouldn't even try before, as well as developing independence when writing words for his assignments.

Conclusion

Visualisation and specific classical music can increase spelling success rates.

Summary

These case studies give an insight into how research can revolutionise the teaching of spelling. The new visualisation method, when integrated with knowledge of the multiple functions of the brain and movement, can give amazing results.

SUCCESS CHART

Write down all the commonly misspelt words that are being learned and write down the date when the word is learnt with the S.P.E.L.L. Method. Place this chart on the wall and celebrate each success.

New Words	*You are a star*		
	Week 1 Date ___ ✓ Tick for correct spelling.	**Week 2 Date** ___ ✓ Tick for correct spelling.	**Week 3 Date** ___ ✓ Tick for correct spelling.

REFERENCES

Ayres, J 1994, *Sensory Integration and the Child,* Western Psychological Services, California.

Bandler, R & Grinder, J 1979, *Frogs into Princes,* Real People Press, Utah.

Blomberg, H & Dempsey, M 2011, *Movements that Heal: Rhythmic Movement Training and Primitive Reflex Integration,* BookPal, Queensland.

Brewer, C & Campbell, D 1992, *Rhythms of Learning: Creative Tools for Developing Lifelong Skills,* Hawker Brownlow, Education Melbourne.

Brooking-Payne, K 1996, *Games Children Play: How Games and Sport Help Children Develop,* Hawthorn Press, UK.

Dennison, P & Dennison, G 1989, *Brain Gym,* Switched on Publication, Queensland.

Goddard, S 1996, *A Teacher's Window into the Child's Mind,* Fern Ridge Press, Oregon.

Goddard Blythe, S 2004, *The Well Balanced Child: Movement and Early Learning,* Hawthorn Press, Gloucestershire.

Goddard Blythe, S 2009, *Attention, Balance and Co-ordination: The A.B.C. of Learning Success,* Wiley-Blackwell, UK.

Hannaford, C 1995, *Smart Moves Why Learning Is Not All In Your Head,* Great Ocean Publishers, Virginia.

Harris, M 1985, 'Visualization and Spelling Competence', *Journal of Developmental Education*, vol. 9, no. 2, pp. 2-5, viewed 21 March 2015, Edu ARTICLES database.

Logan, J, Olson, M & Lindsay, T 1987, 'Editorial Comment: Guest Commentary: Orthographic Awareness Of Highly Successful Spellers', *Journal of Reading Psychology,* vol. 8, no. 2, pp. 3-5, viewed 20 March 2015, Edu ARTICLES database.

Nash-Wortham, M & Hunt, J 2003, *Take Time: Movement Exercises for parents, teachers and therapists of children with difficulties in speaking, reading, writing and spelling,* The Robinswood Press, England.

McAllen, A 1998, *The Extra Lesson: Movement Drawing, and Painting Exercises to Help Children with Difficulties in Writing, Reading and Arithmetic,* Rudolf Steiner College Press, UK.

McAllen, A 2002, *Teaching Children Handwriting,* Rudolf Steiner College Press, USA.

McAllen, A 2004, *Reading Children's Drawings,* Rudolf Steiner College Press, USA.

Murphy, M 2004, 'Spelling Difficulties', *Dyslexia: An Explanation,* Flyleaf Press, UK, viewed 4 April 2015, Link dyslexia@bay.

Peters, M 1985, *Spelling: Caught or Taught? A New Look,* Routledge and Kegan Paul, London.

Rose, C 1985, *Accelerated Learning,* Accelerated Learning Systems, England.

Steiner, R 1966, *Study of Man,* Rudolf Steiner Press, London.

Wade, J 1990, *Super Study: A New Age Study Guide,* Dellastra Pty Ltd, Victoria.

Westwood, P 2104, 'Spelling: do the eyes have it?', *Australia Journal of Learning Difficulties,* vol. 20, no. 1, pp. 3-13, viewed 30 August 2015, Edu ARTICLES database.

Zillmer, E & Spiers, M 2001, *Principles of Neuropsychology,* Wadsworth, USA.

ABOUT MARGARET

Hi, I'm Margaret Harley, an Education Specialist/Therapist who has spent many years discovering new ways to assist children and adults to learn easily despite learning difficulties.

My education began with my *Diploma of Primary Education,* and extended to *Special Education and Literacy.* As my passion is working with children with learning difficulties, I extended my knowledge to encompass accelerated learning, and through NLP techniques, I discovered a wonderful way to spell easily. After six terms in a primary school working with underachieving students, I collated the results and was amazed that there was a 79% average success rate over six terms. I was so inspired and excited with the simple and easy method that I wrote this book *Spell Better in just 5minutes a day*

I also became aware of the educational practices of Rudolf Steiner and I discovered a new perspective and holistic approach to education through my *Associate Diploma of Rudolf Steiner Education.* I attended Educational Kinesiology workshops and discovered that many children have learning blocks through inaccurate processing of sensory information. I enrolled in the *Certificate in Threefold Therapy for Learning* and started applying an exercise program with children with learning difficulties. My fascination with sound and its links to learning resulted in a new role as a practitioner for Integrated Listening Systems. I always wanted to further my expertise so I extended my knowledge with workshops at the Institute for Neuro-Physiological Psychology, Rhythmic Movement Training, and Bilateral Integration Training.

I commenced my own education business, *Learn Easily,* in 1998, and since then hundreds of children with learning difficulties have been assisted, many therapists have participated in the professional development course, and my business has extended.

It has been a wonderful journey to assist so many to learn easily.

CPSIA information can be obtained
at www.ICGtesting.com
Printed in the USA
LVOW12s0524140418
573474LV00002B/320/P